A BOOK ABOUT FARTS

K.J. MACKAY

Welcome to a world filled with laughter, curiosity, and some surprising, air-raising adventures! Get ready for a journey that will take you deep into the mysteries of the human body, exploring one of its most amusing and perplexing phenomena, farts!

You might be wondering why a book about farts? Well, because farts are not just funny noises that make us giggle. They are a natural part of being human. Every single person on this planet experiences them, and they can teach us a lot about how our bodies work.

In this book we are going to dive headfirst into the world of toots, poots, and parps, we will learn fascinating facts, share hilarious jokes, and enjoy delightful watercolour illustrations that will make you chuckle even harder.

So, are you ready to embark on this gas-tastic adventure? Buckle up and prepare for a journey full of surprises and laughter as we explore the wonderful, wacky world of farts together. Let's start this incredible journey on the very next page, where the fun, and the gas begin!.

HAVE YOU EVER WONDERED WHY YOU FART? FARTING IS A WAY FOR YOUR BODY TO RELEASE A GAS BUILD UP. WHEN YOUR BODY DIGESTS FOOD (BREAKS IT DOWN) IT PRODUCES GAS AS PART OF THE PROCESS. ONCE GAS HAS BUILT UP INSIDE THE BODY, IT NEEDS A WAY TO ESCAPE, SO IT ESCAPES AS BURPS AND FARTS! WHEN YOU SWALLOW THINGS LIKE SALIVA, FOOD OR DRINK, YOU ALSO SWALLOW SMALL AMOUNTS OF AIR, AND THIS BUILDS UP IN YOUR BODY. IF YOU ARE NOT FAST ENOUGH TO LET IT OUT AS A BURP, THEN IT MAKES ITS WAY DOWN AND COMES OUT AS A FART TOO!

THERE ARE A FEW THINGS THAT WILL MAKE YOU FART MORE THAN YOU USUALLY WOULD. BEANS ARE FART MAKERS. THEY CONTAIN SOMETHING CALLED RAFFINOSE, WHICH IS A SUGAR THAT THE BODY HAS TROUBLE DIGESTING. RAFFINOSE GOES THROUGH THE SMALL INTESTINE INTO THE LARGE INTESTINE WHERE GOOD BACTERIA HELP BREAK IT DOWN. WHEN THE BACTERIA HELPS BREAK IT DOWN, IT PRODUCES HYDROGEN, CARBON DIOXIDE AND METHANE GASES. THESE GASES THEN NEED TO ESCAPE, SO YOU GUESSED IT, THEY ESCAPE AS FARTS!

WHOLE GRAINS LIKE WHEAT AND OATS NOT ONLY CONTAIN RAFFINOSE, THEY ALSO CONTAIN FIBRE AND STARCH. THESE THINGS ARE BROKEN DOWN IN THE LARGE INTESTINE TOO, CAUSING GAS THAT MAKES YOU FART.

FRUITS LIKE APPLES, PEARS, PEACHES AND EVEN PRUNES CONTAIN A NATURAL SUGAR CALLED SORBITOL. BACTERIA BREAK SORBITOL DOWN IN THE LARGE INTESTINE JUST LIKE RAFFINOSE, CAUSING MORE GASES LEADING TO MORE FARTS!

DID YOU KNOW THAT CHEWING GUM CAN ALSO MAKE YOU FART? WHEN YOU CHEW GUM, YOU ALSO SWALLOW A LOT OF EXCESS AIR. THIS AIR THEN NEEDS TO ESCAPE AND IF YOU'RE NOT FAST ENOUGH TO LET IT OUT AS A BURP, IT MAKES ITS WAY DOWN TO YOUR BUTT AND COMES OUT AS A FART!

DAIRY CONTAINS SOMETHING CALLED LACTOSE, A LOT OF PEOPLE HAVE TROUBLE DIGESTING LACTOSE. IT'S BECAUSE THEY DON'T HAVE ENOUGH OF AN ENZYME CALLED LACTASE WHICH HELPS DIGEST THE LACTOSE. SO WHEN YOU STRUGGLE TO DIGEST LACTOSE, IT LEADS TO YOU FEELING BLOATED AND HAVING GAS.

FIZZY DRINKS CAN ALSO MAKE YOU GASSY. ALL THOSE BUBBLES LEAD TO A LOT OF EXTRA GAS, AND THAT GAS ESCAPES AS BURPS AND FARTS!

ITS A WELL KNOW FACT THAT FARTS SMELL! SOME A LOT MORE THAN OTHERS. SMELLY FARTS HAVE A LOT TO DO WITH WHAT YOU EAT. SOMETIMES THE DIGESTION PROCESS CREATES HYDROGEN SULPHIDE, THIS GAS SMELLS LIKE ROTTEN EGGS AND CAN MAKE YOUR FARTS SUPER STINKY! HIGH SULPHUR FOODS CAUSE YOU TO HAVE FARTS SO SMELLY THAT THEY CLEAR A ROOM IN SECONDS. BROCCOLI, BRUSSELS SPROUTS, CAULIFLOWER, AND CABBAGE ARE ALL HIGH SULPHUR FOODS, BUT THEY'RE NOT THE ONLY ONES. GARLIC, GRAINS, MEATS, ONIONS AND NUTS ALSO HELP CONTRIBUTE TO SMELLY FARTS

FART JOKES

Q. WHAT DO YOU CALL A GHOST FART?

A. SPIRIT BOMB.

Q. WHY WON'T THE SKELETON FART IN PUBLIC?

A. HE DOESN'T HAVE THE GUTS

Q. WHY DID THE MAN STOP TELLING FART JOKES?

A. HE WAS TOLD THAT HIS JOKES STINK.

Q. WHY DID THE CHICKEN CROSS THE ROAD?

A. SHE DIDN'T WANT THE OTHER CHICKENS TO NOTICE THAT SHE FARTED.

Q. WHY DID THE FART MISS GRADUATION?

A. IT GOT EXPELLED.

Q. WHAT DO YOU CALL A DINOSAUR FART?

A. A BLAST FROM THE PAST!

Q. WHAT DO YOU GET IF YOU EAT BEANS WITH ONIONS?

A. TEARGAS!

Q. WHAT DO YOU CALL A CAT WHO LIKES TO EAT BEANS?

A. PUSS 'N' TOOTS!

What should you do when you fart? Well, that really depends where you are, who's around, and if anyone actually notices that you have farted. First of all, don't be embarrassed, everyone farts!! That's right everyone! Your teacher, your parents, the neighbour, even the neighbour's dog. Holding in a fart when you need to can cause bloating and a sore tummy, so it's best to let them out when they come along. There are a few things you can do to make it a little less embarrassing and a lot more polite. First, if you can leave the room, then you should. Quietly exit the room, cut the cheese where no one is around, and then return like nothing happened… perfect! There are, however, times when there is no way to leave. So, if you can't leave the room but want to let that ripper out, it is polite to say pardon me or excuse me after you have done it. It's also polite to own up to a fart if someone says something about it. If someone asked you if you farted, and you did, just say yes and carry on with whatever you were doing. Honesty is the best policy, even when it comes to farts. If you're just at home and you're feeling gassy, then let them out wherever and whenever you like, as long as it's not at one of mum's very fancy dinner parties, you are good to go.

HAVE YOU EVER WONDERED WHAT HAPPENS IF YOU FART WHEN YOU ARE WEARING A WETSUIT? WELL, IF YOU ARE DOWN IN THE WATER AND YOU HAVE A WETSUIT ON AND YOU SUDDENLY FART, THEN THE GAS HAS TO FIND A WAY OUT. A WETSUIT HAS FIVE OPENINGS, THE TWO ARMS, THE TWO LEGS AND THE HEAD. BECAUSE THE HEAD IS USUALLY THE HIGHEST POINT OF THE SUIT, THE FART WILL MAKE ITS WAY UP AND OUT THE BACK BEHIND YOUR NECK. THEN YOU CAN WATCH THE FART BUBBLE FLOAT AWAY! BECAUSE GAS IS LIGHTER THAN WATER (AND YOUR FART IS, OF COURSE, GAS) YOU CAN WATCH YOUR FART BUBBLE FLOAT ALL THE WAY TO THE SURFACE. HOW COOL IS THAT?!

WHAT HAPPENS WHEN YOU HOLD IN A FART INSTEAD OF LETTING IT OUT? IF YOU ARE HOLDING IN A FART, IT CAN ADD PRESSURE TO YOUR DIGESTIVE SYSTEM, THIS CAUSES A NUMBER OF PROBLEMS. THE TRAPPED GAS ADDS PRESSURE TO YOUR MUSCLES IN YOUR ABDOMEN AND THIS CAN CAUSE YOU PAIN. THE MORE GAS YOU HOLD IN, THE WORSE THE PAIN. EXTRA GAS AND AIR IN THE STOMACH CAN CAUSE YOU TO BLOAT (THIS IS WHEN THE STOMACH SWELLS AND FEELS FULL AND UNCOMFORTABLE). SOMETIMES YOU CAN EVEN FEEL THE GAS BUBBLING AND GURGLING AROUND YOUR STOMACH!

THE MORE YOU TRY TO HOLD IN THE GAS, THE HARDER IT GETS TO HOLD IT IN. NOT ONLY IS IT GOING TO BE UNCOMFORTABLE, EVENTUALLY THAT FART IS GOING TO MAKE ITS WAY OUT. SO MY ADVICE IS, IF YOU FEEL A FART BREWING, BE READY TO LET THAT RIPPER OUT!

FUN FACTS

THERE ARE MANY NAMES FOR A FART, WHILE THE SCIENTIFIC TERM FOR FARTING IS FLATULENCE HERE ARE SOME NOT SO SCIENTIFIC TERMS FOR IT: CUTTING THE CHEESE, PASSING GAS, BLOWING OFF, FARTING, FLUFFING, TOOTING, AIR BISCUIT AND BOTTOM BURP.

RICE IS THE ONLY WHOLE GRAIN THAT DOESN'T CAUSE FARTS.

DINOSAURS USE TO FART, AND THEY FARTED A LOT!!

ADULTS FART ABOUT 14 TIMES A DAY.

FARTS SMELL WORSE IN THE SHOWER.

BIRDS DON'T FART.

THE WORLD'S OLDEST JOKE IS A FART JOKE.

WOMEN'S FARTS SMELL WORSE THAN MEN'S.

YOU FART MORE WHEN YOU ARE FLYING IN AN AEROPLANE.

WHY DO SPICY FOODS MAKE YOUR FARTS FEEL HOT? WELL, THAT'S A VERY GOOD QUESTION! SPICY FOODS CONTAIN THINGS LIKE CAPSICUM AND CHILLI, WHICH MAKES YOU MOUTH SUPER HOT WHEN EATING THEM, NOT ONLY DO THEY MAKE YOUR MOUTH HOT BUT WHEN THEY COME OUT THEY MAKE THE SKIN ON YOUR BUM HOT, MAKING IT FEEL LIKE YOU'RE DOING A HOT FART! WANT TO AVOID THOSE HOT FARTS? THEN TRY HAVING A POOP AFTER YOU'VE EATEN THE SPICY FOOD, THIS USUALLY REDUCES SYMPTOMS OF HOT AND SPICY FARTS.

SOMETHING ELSE THAT MAKES YOUR FARTS FEEL WARM IS WEARING TIGHT CLOTHES, THE FART GETS TRAPPED AND LINGERS AROUND FOR LONGER, MAKING YOUR FART FEEL WARM. FOOD INTOLERANCE CAN ALSO MAKE YOUR FARTS FEEL WARM. IF YOU'RE EATING SOMETHING THAT DOESN'T AGREE WITH YOU, IT NOT ONLY CAUSES HOT FARTS, IT CAN ALSO CAUSE DIARRHEA AND AN UPSET STOMACH.

You fart in your sleep! That's right, while you're fast asleep, you let out gassy little bum bubbles, and you don't even realise! But if you let out a real ripper, there's a chance that the noise of the fart could actually wake you up. When you sleep, all the muscles in your body relax, and that lets farts slip out very easily. Farting in your sleep is completely normal, but if you would like to cut down on the amount of farting you do through the night, there are a few things that you can do. First of all, make sure that you are not eating too close to bedtime. The later you eat, the more food you will have left undigested, and that means more farts. Sleeping on your left side is proven to help digestion, so something as simple as switching the side you sleep on could help reduce those night time farts. Lastly, stay away from those fizzy drinks later in the day. Not only will all the sugar in them make it harder for you to get to sleep, but all those bubbles will have you farting up a storm in dreamland. So there you have it, a few easy ways to cut down the nighttime farts, and remember, everyone farts in their sleep!

RIDDLE: SOMETIMES I AM BORN IN SILENCE, OTHER TIMES, NO. I AM UNSEEN, BUT I MAKE MY PRESENCE KNOWN. IN TIME, I FADE WITHOUT A TRACE. I HARM NO ONE, BUT I AM UNPOPULAR WITH ALL. WHAT AM I?

ANSWER: A FART

FUN FACTS

FARTS CAN TRAVEL AT ABOUT 10 FEET PER SECOND, THAT'S APPROXIMATELY 6.8 MILES PER HOUR.

A SCIENTIST THAT STUDIES FARTS IS CALLED A FLATOLOGIST.

THE FIRST FART JOKE DATES ALL THE WAY BACK TO 1900 BC.

SCIENTISTS HAVE FOUND THAT THE VOLUME OF A FART CAN VARY FROM AS SMALL AS 17ML TOO AS BIG AS 375ML.

THE LONGEST RECORDED FART WAS ACHIEVED BY A MAN NAMED BERNARD CLEMMENS FROM LONDON AND IT WAS A 2 MINUTE AND 48 SECOND CONTINUOUS FART ON MAY 17, 2016.

THE LOUDEST FART EVER RECORDED WAS DONE BY ALVIN MESHITS IN MADELINE, TEXAS. THE FART MAINTAINED A LEVEL OF 194 DECIBELS FOR ONE THIRD OF A SECOND ON MAY 16, 1972.

IF YOU FARTED IN COLD AIR WITH YOU PANTS DOWN, YOU WOULD BE ABLE TO SEE IT, JUST LIKE YOU CAN SEE YOUR BREATH ON A VERY COLD DAY.

SLOTHS DON'T FART.

IF YOU ARE NOT A FAN OF FARTS, OR ARE GOING SOMEWHERE NICE AND WOULD LIKE TO KEEP YOUR FARTING TO A MINIMUM, THEN THERE ARE SOME THINGS YOU CAN DO TO REDUCE THE AMOUNT YOU FART.

1. CUT OUT CHEWING GUM. WHEN YOU CHEW GUM, YOU SWALLOW MORE AIR THAN YOU USUALLY WOULD, AND THAT AIR HAS TO ESCAPE SOMEHOW. BY NOT CHEWING GUM, YOU CAN REDUCE EXCESS AIR, THEREFORE REDUCING THE AMOUNT YOU FART.
2. EATING SMALLER MEALS MORE OFTEN CAN HELP REDUCE THE AMOUNT OF WORK YOUR DIGESTIVE SYSTEM HAS TO DO, THIS REDUCES THE AMOUNT YOU FART
3. TAKING REGULAR PROBIOTICS (PROBIOTICS ARE GOOD BACTERIA THAT HELP KEEP YOU HEALTHY) CAN HELP REDUCE WIND.
4. EXERCISE! THIS IS A GREAT WAY TO GET FOOD MOVING THROUGH YOUR STOMACH, PLUS IF YOU'RE OUT FOR A WALK, YOU CAN LET OUT AS MANY FARTS AS YOU LIKE AND HARDLY ANYONE WILL NOTICE!
5. THE FASTER YOU EAT AND DRINK, THE MORE AIR YOU LET IN, SO SLOWING DOWN THE SPEED YOU EAT CAN ACTUALLY REDUCE THE AMOUNT YOU FART.

SCIENTISTS HAVE CREATED A DATABASE OF ANIMALS THAT FART. THAT'S RIGHT, THAT MEANS SCIENTISTS ARE STUDYING ANIMALS FARTING! FASCINATING RIGHT!

SO EXACTLY WHAT ANIMALS FART?

WELL SEALS, LIONS, BATS AND EVEN BEARDED DRAGONS ALL FART, AND IF YOU HAVE A PET DOG, YOU KNOW THAT THEY CAN FART!

WOMBATS NOT ONLY FART, BUT WHEN THEY POOP IT COMES OUT SQUARE!

RATS CAN FART, BUT THEY CAN'T BURP!

SO WHAT ANIMALS CAN'T FART?

BIRDS, CLAMS, SALAMANDERS AND FROGS ALL DON'T FART. BADGERS HAVE SOME OF THE MOST DISGUSTING POOP IN THE ANIMAL KINGDOM, BUT AS OF NOW THEY HAVE NOT BEEN RECORDED FARTING, THAT'S NOT TO SAY THAT THEY CAN'T, BUT NO ONE HAS CAUGHT A BADGER FARTING YET!

SCIENTISTS IN AUSTRALIA CONDUCTED AN EXPERIMENT TO SEE IF THEY COULD SPREAD GERMS THROUGH FARTING. THEY HAD A TEST SUBJECT FART INTO TWO PETRI DISHES FROM A DISTANCE OF 5 CENTIMETRES. FOR THE FIRST FART, HE WAS FULLY CLOTHED AND FOR THE SECOND ONE; HE HAD HIS BOTTOM EXPOSED. THEY THEN WATCHED TO SEE WHAT HAPPENED OVERNIGHT. THE SECOND PETRI DISH SPROUTED VISIBLE LUMPS. IT WAS TWO DIFFERENT TYPES OF BACTERIA THAT ARE USUALLY FOUND IN THE STOMACH AND ON THE SKIN. THE FIRST PETRI DISH HAD NOTHING. THE CLOTHES HAD ACTED AS A FILTER. AMAZING! DON'T PANIC THOUGH, THE TYPES OF BACTERIA THAT WERE FOUND IN THE SECOND DISH WERE COMPLETELY HARMLESS AND WERE VERY SIMILAR TO THE FRIENDLY BACTERIA THAT YOU FIND IN YOGHURT. WHAT AN EXPERIMENT!

HERE IS PROBABLY THE WEIRDEST FACT YOU WILL FIND IN THIS ENTIRE BOOK, AND MANY OTHER BOOKS TOO!

IN FLORIDA USA IT IS ILLEGAL TO FART IN A PUBLIC PLACE AFTER 6PM... BUT ONLY ON A THURSDAY. YES, YOU READ THAT RIGHT! NO FARTING IN PUBLIC AFTER 6PM ON THURSDAYS! AS FAR AS WE KNOW, NO ONE HAS BEEN ARRESTED OR FINED FOR THIS, AND IT MUST BE A VERY, VERY, VERY OLD LAW, BUT IT'S STILL A LAW!

I TOLD YOU, THAT'S ONE WEIRD FACT!

LET US ANSWER A QUESTION WE KNOW YOU HAVE ALL BEEN WONDERING ABOUT, DO FISH FART? WELL, A FART IS THE BODY RELEASING GASES FROM THE BEHIND AFTER DIGESTION, SO TECHNICALLY NO, FISH, DO NOT FART! SOMETIMES IF YOU WATCH FISH, YOU CAN SEE AIR ESCAPING FROM THEIR BODY (AND THEIR BUM) AND FLOATING OFF IN BUBBLES. HOWEVER, THIS IS AIR, AND NOT A GAS OR BYPRODUCT OF DIGESTION AND THEREFORE NOT A FART. THE EXPERTS SAY THAT THE GASES CAUSED BY DIGESTION IN FISH ARE CONSOLIDATED WITH THEIR POOP AND RELEASED FROM THEIR BODIES IN A JELLY LIKE TUBE, THAT FISH WILL ACTUALLY SOMETIMES EAT, EEWWWWW!! IT'S GROSS, BUT IT'S CERTAINLY NOT A FART.

CAN ASTRONAUTS FART IN SPACE? YES, THEY CAN! AND BECAUSE OF THE LACK OF GRAVITY, THEY ACTUALLY TEND TO FART MORE THAT THEY WOULD DOWN HERE ON EARTH. WHILE FARTING IN SPACE CAN'T REALLY DO TOO MUCH DAMAGE, IF THERE WAS A SMALL FIRE AND YOU WERE TO FART YOU WOULD INTRODUCE GASES LIKE METHANE AND HYDROGEN WHICH ARE FLAMMABLE, AND COULD POSSIBLY MAKE THE SMALL FIRE WORSE, ASIDE FROM THAT THERE REALLY AREN'T TOO MANY RISKS FARTING IN SPACE. UNFORTUNATELY, BECAUSE THERE IS A LACK OF AIRFLOW IN SPACE, IF YOU WERE TO FART, THE SMELL WOULD LINGER AROUND FOR QUITE SOME TIME. SO IF YOU EVER TRAVEL TO SPACE, IT PAYS TO REMEMBER THAT THE BEST PLACE TO FART UP THERE IS IN THE BATHROOM, WHERE THERE IS A LITTLE MORE AIRFLOW AND SO YOU ARE AWAY FROM OTHERS THAT WOULD HAVE TO SMELL THAT FART FOR A FAIRLY LONG TIME.

FART JOKES

Q. WHAT DO YOU CALL A FARTING FAIRY?

A. STINKER BELL.

Q. WHY SHOULD YOU NEVER FART IN AN ELEVATOR?

A. IT'S WRONG ON SO MANY LEVELS.

Q. WHAT'S INVISIBLE AND SMELLS LIKE CARROTS?

A. A BUNNY FART!

Q. WHY DID THE MECHANIC FART?

A. THE CAR HE WAS WORKING ON JUST NEEDED A LITTLE GAS.

Q. WHY ARE APPLE STORE EMPLOYEES NEVER ALLOWED TO FART AT WORK?

A. THEY HAVE NO WINDOWS.

KNOCK KNOCK

WHO'S THERE?

SMELL.

SMELL WHO?

SMELL YA LATER, I'M OUTTA HERE!

IN CHINA, THERE ARE PEOPLE THAT WORK AS PROFESSIONAL FART SMELLERS, AND THEY EARN A FAIR BIT OF MONEY TO DO IT TOO. THERE ARE SOME ALTERNATIVE MEDICINE PRACTITIONERS THAT BELIEVE YOU CAN FIND OUT WHAT'S WRONG WITH SOMEONE JUST BY SMELLING THEIR FARTS, SO THIS IS WHAT THEY DO. THEY BELIEVE THEY CAN DIAGNOSE AN ILLNESS BY WHETHER THE FARTS SMELL, SALTY, SWEET, BITTER, SAVOURY, FISHY OR MEATY. AND WHEN YOU THINK ABOUT IT, IT'S ACTUALLY NOT THAT FAR-FETCHED. DOGS CAN DETECT ILLNESSES AND DISEASES JUST BY SMELLING PEOPLE, SO THERE'S REALLY NOTHING TO SAY IT DOESN'T WORK FOR PEOPLE TRAINED THE RIGHT WAY TOO. TO HAVE A JOB AS AN OFFICIAL FART SMELLER YOU HAVE TO BE BETWEEN THE AGES OF 18-45, HAVE NO NASAL DEFECTS (NO PROBLEMS WITH YOUR NOSE OR SMELLING), NOT DRINK ALCOHOL AND OF COURSE BE ABLE TO STAND THE SMELL OF FARTS! NOW THAT'S A STINKER OF A JOB.

IN THE 1600'S SOME DOCTORS WOULD RECOMMEND TO THEIR PATIENTS THAT THEY FART INTO JARS AND SAVE THEM, THEN WHEN THEY WERE EXPOSED TO THE BUBONIC PLAGUE THEY SHOULD SMELL THE FARTS IN THE JARS TO HELP TREAT IT. THEY BELIEVED THAT THE AIR POLLUTED WITH THE PLAGUE COULD BE DILUTED WITH SOMETHING EQUALLY AS POTENT TO REDUCE THE CHANCE OF CATCHING THE ILLNESS. IT'S SAFE TO SAY THAT SMELLING FARTS IN A JAR PROBABLY DIDN'T STOP ANYONE FROM CATCHING THE PLAGUE, HOWEVER THE THOUGHT THAT IT MIGHT HELP COULD HAVE REALLY HELPED TO CALM PEOPLES NERVES.

CONGRATULATIONS! YOU HAVE REACHED THE END OF THE BOOK. YOU HAVE LEARNT EVERYTHING THERE IS TO KNOW ABOUT FARTS! NOW YOU HAVE SOME AWESOME FART FACTS TO SHARE WITH YOUR FRIENDS AND FAMILY!

WHEREVER YOU MAY BE, LET THE WIND BLOW FREE.

(c) 2023, K.J. MACKAY

ALL RIGHTS RESERVED. NO PART OF THIS PUBLICATION MAY BE REPRODUCED, DISTRIBUTED, OR TRANSMITTED IN ANY FORM OR BY ANY MEANS, INCLUDING PHOTOCOPYING, RECORDING, OR OTHER ELECTRONIC OR MECHANICAL METHODS, WITHOUT THE PRIOR WRITTEN PERMISSION OF THE PUBLISHER, EXCEPT IN THE CASE OF BRIEF QUOTATIONS EMBODIED IN CRITICAL REVIEWS AND CERTAIN OTHER NONCOMMERCIAL USES PERMITTED BY COPYRIGHT LAW.

THE INFORMATION PROVIDED IN "A BOOK ABOUT FARTS" IS INTENDED FOR ENTERTAINMENT AND EDUCATIONAL PURPOSES ONLY. WHILE EFFORTS HAVE BEEN MADE TO ENSURE THE ACCURACY AND COMPLETENESS OF THE INFORMATION PRESENTED, THE AUTHOR AND PUBLISHER MAKE NO REPRESENTATIONS OR WARRANTIES REGARDING THE COMPREHENSIVENESS OR ACCURACY OF THE CONTENT. READERS ARE ENCOURAGED TO CONSULT WITH MEDICAL PROFESSIONALS OR EXPERTS FOR ANY SPECIFIC HEALTH-RELATED CONCERNS OR QUESTIONS.

THE JOKES AND HUMOR IN THIS BOOK ARE INTENDED TO BE LIGHTHEARTED AND FUN. THEY ARE NOT MEANT TO OFFEND OR HARM ANY INDIVIDUALS OR GROUPS. THE AUTHOR AND PUBLISHER DISCLAIM ANY LIABILITY FOR ANY POTENTIAL CONSEQUENCES RESULTING FROM THE USE OR MISUSE OF THE INFORMATION, JOKES, OR CONTENT CONTAINED IN THIS BOOK.

READING "A BOOK ABOUT FARTS" IS A VOLUNTARY CHOICE, AND INDIVIDUALS SHOULD USE THEIR DISCRETION WHEN DECIDING WHETHER TO ENGAGE WITH ITS CONTENT. THE AUTHOR AND PUBLISHER SHALL NOT BE HELD RESPONSIBLE FOR ANY INTERPRETATIONS, ACTIONS, OR CONSEQUENCES RESULTING FROM THE READING OR USE OF THIS BOOK.

PLEASE REMEMBER THAT FARTING, WHILE A NATURAL BODILY FUNCTION, SHOULD BE PRACTICED WITH COURTESY AND CONSIDERATION FOR OTHERS IN SOCIAL SETTINGS. ENJOY THE HUMOR AND EDUCATIONAL ASPECTS OF THIS BOOK RESPONSIBLY AND WITH A SENSE OF HUMOR!